Luna & Lola

Luna & Lola

Priscilla Rattazzi

WITH AN ESSAY BY CHRIS WHITTLE

CALLAWAY

New York

2010

In memory of my mother,

S USANNA A GNELLI ,

who taught me to appreciate beauty and irony

BORN A PRIL 22, 1922

DIED M AY 15, 2009

CONTENTS

I always thought the world was divided into two types of people: those who liked dogs and those who didn't, and that those who liked dogs either liked big ones or small ones. I preferred big ones.

In 1997 my family got a golden retriever. Seven years later (after much resistance on my part), we got a miniature dachshund.

Our family became a rare breed: we ultimately discovered that we loved having both sizes. After a rough start, our dogs, Luna and Lola, became friends and the funniest couple in Carnegie Hill.

These are their stories.

Luna

THE PUSH for a dog started in the early nineties when my son, Maxi, was about six years old and my daughter Andrea was two.

"Mom, can we get a dog?" asked Maxi.

"Maybe," I replied, having already learned that saying yes to a child too quickly was almost always a bad idea.

A couple of years later, the question became more of a never-ending refrain.

"Let me think about it," I replied every time the dog plea popped up. But the refrain continued.

In the fall of 1994, after I became pregnant with my daughter Sasha, we sold our apartment on the West Side and bought a townhouse in New York City's Carnegie Hill neighborhood. The dog plea had abated with the move, but about a year later my children started again.

"We need to get a dog," said Maxi, looking me straight in the eye. "For real."

This time, I had to relent.

I don't think my husband, Chris, or I worried that a dog would introduce chaos at that point. There was so much of it already with three children that we thought, perhaps foolishly, a dog would not make that much of a difference.

We found an ad in the paper for golden retriever puppies. ONLY TWO LEFT, it read. Six weeks later, on a beautiful June day in 1997, Maxi, Andrea, and I brought one of those puppies home. We named her Luna, which means moon in Italian.

I had never trained a dog before and wasn't sure where to begin. I was overwhelmed, not to mention the fact that I had three small children to raise.

Eventually, I started to get the hang of it. I quickly learned that standing on a pile of paper towels thrown over a lot of club soda would remove most stains from anywhere.

By the spring of 1999, when Luna turned two, she was finally house-trained and reliable. We spent most weekends in East Hampton. Luna quickly became the best playmate the children had ever had. They would dress her up for Easter, Halloween, and Christmas; try to ride her like a horse; swim with her in the pool; and sleep with her in their bedrooms, where she would occasionally wake them with her whimpering dreams.

Luna was the quintessential water dog. Everyone threw her tennis balls on the lawn, in the pond, and in the ocean. We often took long walks along Georgica Beach, and when we got to Georgica Pond she would always dive in to cool off.

Sometimes I would sail to the beach with Luna. She would get so excited as we neared the shore that she would jump off the boat and swim the rest of the way. If I went in the ocean, she would always come with me.

When Luna became tired, she would sit and smell the sea air while holding her nose high into the breeze, as regal as any queen.

Lola

ATT THE END of the summer of 2002, Andrea and Sasha became very vocal about wanting a second dog. Their brother had just gone away to school, and I think they really missed him. The new refrain became, "We want a little dog we can hold, who can sit on our laps and sleep on our beds."

I was dead set against this. "I don't like small dogs," I said. "Small dogs bark because they have an inferiority complex."

The Internet had become the most common way to buy puppies. One afternoon I arrived home to find my daughters beckoning me to the computer. "Mama! We found a website with miniature dachshunds. Look at that one; her name is Thumbelina. Can we get her, *please*?"

A few days later Chris took me aside and told me he thought we should get the puppy. "It will mean a lot to our daughters," he argued.

"Of course it will," I said sarcastically, "but I will end up doing all the work!" (Which, of course, is exactly what happened.)

I had very mixed feelings about a small dog. The mere idea of a yapping creature sent chills down my spine. And the thought of house-training another animal—given that small dogs were harder to train than large ones—seemed daunting. On the other hand, Luna had just turned seven and was showing signs of slowing down. I thought a companion might energize her.

After much debate, we decided to get a black miniature dachshund. *What am I getting myself into?* I couldn't help but wonder.

On April 1, 2004, I drove to Newark Airport to meet the newest member of our family. She was flown Delta Air Cargo and arrived from Alabama via Atlanta. (I suspect the trip might have traumatized her for life.)

The attendants at the terminal handed me a tiny crate, and I opened it and peeked inside. Gazing back at me with an expression of absolute terror, I saw what looked like a shivering peanut. She was the smallest and cutest thing I had ever seen. I took her in my arms, wrapped her in a warm blanket, and held her close. She shook all the way home, and by the time we got there I was in love.

After many discussions, we named her Lola. It worked well with Luna.

Lola didn't last very long sleeping downstairs by herself. Despite the fact that she had really short legs, she quickly figured out how to jump over the fence I had built for her. I'm not sure how she did it, but every time little Lola jumped, she looked like a kangaroo.

Within weeks she went from a crate downstairs to a crate upstairs to sleeping on our beds rolled up like a donut. We figured out that she liked to burrow, so we covered her up with a blanket; this made her nights (and ours) infinitely more peaceful.

I never really thought of Lola as a dog. She was more like a bird, a cross between a penguin and a duck. Her pitter-patter was immediately endearing, and her intelligence quite obvious.

As for her incessant yapping, I learned to tune it out and it stopped bothering me.

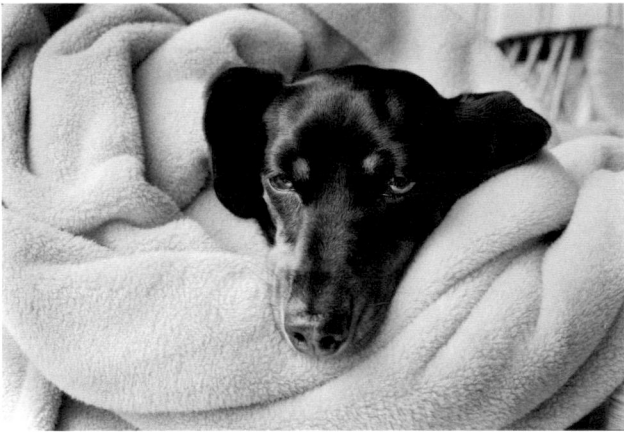

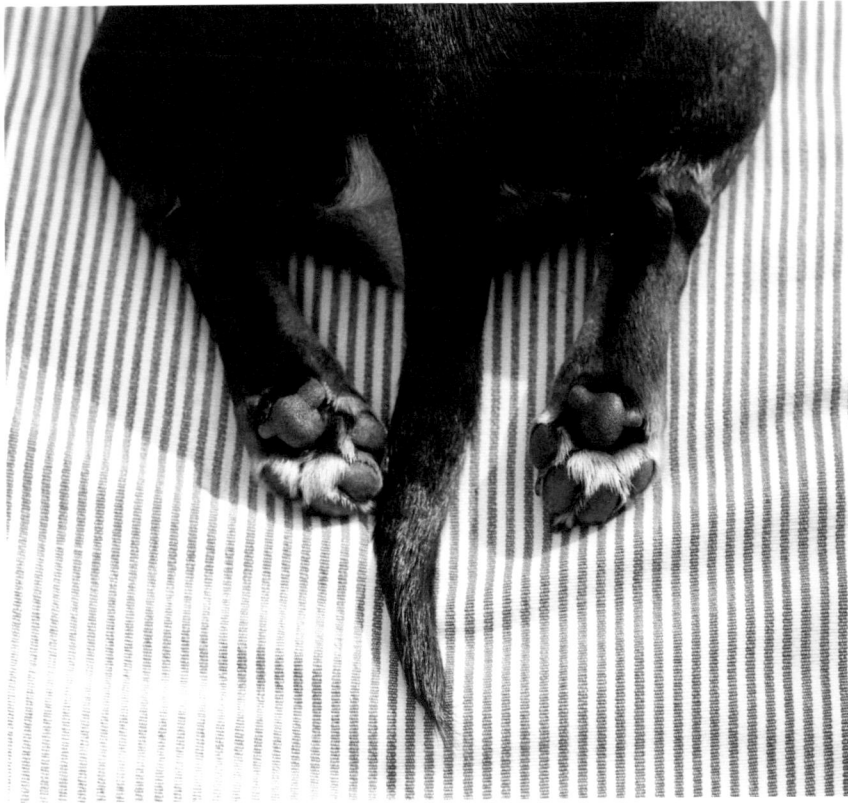

Luna
&Lola

NEEDLESS TO SAY, Luna was not happy when Lola arrived. She would run away anytime Lola would try to play with her. Lola had probably decided that Luna was her new mother. Luna, on the other hand, would have none of it; it was hate at first sight.

Lola's behavior didn't help things. She was always trying to bite Luna's tail; never quite managing to hold on to it for long before Luna would shake her off with the most disdainful annoyance. I wish I could've explained to Luna that one day they would become friends and keep each other company.

After a while Luna accepted Lola, and I breathed a sigh of relief.

They started playing together, and watching them tussle made me laugh out loud. I dubbed it The Luna and Lola Show. I decided it had to become *Luna & Lola* the book.

Strangers in Central Park would smile when they saw me walking Luna and Lola together. I would return their grins, grateful for the comic relief this unlikely pair had added to my life.

They were the ultimate odd couple—not just physically. In the summer, Luna adored the ocean while Lola was terrified of it. Luna was always in the shade while Lola basked in the sun. Luna loved being photographed and Lola hated it. She would run away anytime I pointed a camera at her. When we went for a walk, Luna could stay out forever. Lola couldn't wait to turn around and head home with her famous determination.

I was so used to having just Luna around, who was the most relaxed dog in the world. She loved everybody and could be petted by anyone at any time. She was a canine saint.

Lola was a terror from the beginning. She barked incessantly at strangers and pretended to bite their ankles as they walked past her. I never thought she would be as high-strung, fearful, and antisocial as she was. She even developed the ability to give us dirty looks if we dared to wake her from a nap.

Still, for all their physical and temperamental differences, they became a team, poignantly devoted and fiercely protective. In New York, it was the doorbell. Why on earth would they start barking before it even rang? In East Hampton, it was the wildlife. I loved watching them run off on coordinated sniffing frenzies, chasing the many deer off our lawn.

Eventually, they would split up according to their instincts. Luna chased birds along the pond while Lola dug rabbit holes.

Luna, Lola, & Us

I SUPPOSE THAT getting a second dog when the first one was starting to get old was a way to fool myself; I thought perhaps Lola would make losing Luna easier.

By 2008, Luna was starting to slow down and seemed tired all the time. Her eyes were getting cloudy with cataracts. She was having trouble going up and down stairs, and we couldn't throw her tennis balls anymore without her limping for days. Dr. Miller, Luna's veterinarian, confirmed that she had arthritis. I sympathized, as my joints were starting to hurt as well.

Not only did I know Luna's time was limited, I also began to dread what her death would mean. I had turned fifty not too long ago, my son was twenty-four and independent, my oldest daughter was heading for college, and my youngest was already in high school. Luna and Lola seemed to represent the shifting reality of my life—which had moved from babies to an almost empty nest and into middle age in the too-brief span of Luna's life.

It's interesting to see how things turned out. My children begged me to get the dogs. They swore they were going to help with all the work, but they rarely did. Then they grew up and started leaving—but the dogs stayed. Their effusive love and wagging tails helped fill the void.

Lola became the new baby of the house. There were no more bottles or strollers, but there was Lola. I loved holding her and stroking her chest.

And it became quite clear that Lola would be the last one to sit on my lap when all my children had gone.

Epilogue

IN EARLY NOVEMBER 2009, I found a lump on Luna's neck, which seemed to have grown overnight. After a biopsy, Dr. Miller called me to deliver the news: Luna had an extremely aggressive form of cancer and had only a few months to live. He had always warned me that golden retrievers lived twelve to fourteen years, and she was almost thirteen.

A week later, Luna had surgery. While operating, they found malignant growths everywhere. After Luna recovered from the operation, I took her to the Animal Medical Center for a sonogram, x rays, and blood work.

The news kept getting worse. She had lesions in her lungs and a mass in her colon. The doctors suggested chemotherapy, but told us that the treatment would only increase her chance of survival by twenty percent.

Chris, always the optimist, thought those odds were good; I disagreed.

Judging from how hard Luna shook during the consultation with the oncologist and how ecstatic she was when I picked her up from a morning of examinations, I didn't think chemo would be the answer, at least not for her. I decided to take her home and just let her be.

By then it was early December. My greatest wish was for Luna to make it through the holidays. But on the morning of December 21, three days after she had stopped eating and had started bleeding internally, I called Dr. Miller and asked him to come.

When he rang the doorbell, my heart sank. We walked towards Luna, who was lying on her bed in our greenhouse, barely able to lift her head. There was an awkward moment of polite conversation while the doctor took the syringes from his bag. He put the first needle of tranquilizer into Luna's back leg. She didn't even flinch. A few minutes later came the second injection, a massive dose of anesthesia that stopped her heart.

To put an end to her suffering was the right thing to do, but right then and there it was utterly devastating. I felt as if a part of me had died. Her life had ended and a major chapter of mine had also come to a close. For the next few months my sadness was kept at bay by the looming deadline of this book.

So here's to you, Luna, and to you, too, little Lola, and here's to all the golden retrievers and little dachshunds living somewhere in this universe.

PRISCILLA RATTAZZI
NEW YORK
FEBRUARY 18, 2010

P.S. On April 29th, 2010, I drove upstate to visit a golden retriever breeder. I met the parents of a new litter born in early April. The mom looked just like Luna and the dad was a carbon copy of Luna's dad. My heart melted. By the end of the visit, I had left a deposit for a new puppy I wasn't even able to see yet.

As this book goes to press, I am smiling at the thought of new life, more tennis balls, and another decade of walks along the shore. How Lola will feel, however, is a different story....

L U N A

LUNA never got the retriever part. For twelve years, thousands upon thousands of tennis balls were hit to her. Not one came back. She gave back in other ways.

For more than four thousand mornings, through the park and by the sea, she walked Priscilla. Like a pair of postmen, neither rain, nor snow, nor sleet kept them from their appointed rounds. Squirrels were chased futilely, fellow dogs sniffed, swans harassed, horse manure eaten with relish. Two miles and a bit every day makes ten thousand miles they walked together. That created a depth of bond known to few.

Luna was a movie star, effortlessly elegant and beautiful. The fluffiest of her litter, she always dressed in rich furs no matter the weather. She was a living pose, a canine supermodel. The planet's most photographed dog, she appeared in books, newspapers, and film.

True to her breed and her birthplace, Southampton, she was of the water: the pond and its darting minnows fascinated her; she was an accidental bodysurfer in ocean waves; and in the pool she would provide without complaint her famous "tail rides," dog paddling furiously with as many as three children in tow.

The arrival of Lola she suffered. She had a brief period of uncharacteristic fluster. You could almost see her saying "what is this black, barking thing that licks my saliva, bites my face, and hangs endlessly on my tail?" Yet, even if Lola did not, Luna mellowed, and later in her life you could catch them sleeping side by side.

Her domain was the lawn of East Hampton. She was happiest there, tearing from the car the moment we arrived. Her memorial rock will be on her "spot," the knoll where she would sit with head regally high watching over her land.

Luna was a member of our family and a friend to our friends. The saying among our circle became "she is a person in a dog suit." She greeted all no matter their mood. Luna was here for whole childhoods and long mid-lives.

She would eat anything, and quickly. Forgetting her pride, Luna would beg, lurking beneath dinner tables, her nose right there where you thought your napkin should be. Luna's appetite was epic, and when it waned we knew her time was near.

In the end, she displayed the dignity and grace that were her hallmarks throughout life. Her serenity touched us all.

We never minded those tennis balls not coming back to us. We wish she could.

CHRIS WHITTLE
NEW YORK
DECEMBER 21, 2009

A C K N O W L E D G M E N T S

Many thanks to:

Nicholas Callaway for believing in this project;

the team at Callaway—Amy Cloud, Cathy Ferrara, Nelson Gómez,

Krupa Jhaveri, and Toshiya Masuda—for being a pleasure to work with;

Laumont Editions, especially Alison Bradshaw, for doing all the technical work

and guiding me through the maze of this new digital world;

Thomas Palmer for his masterful rendition of these images into ink on paper;

Meridian for printing the book;

Susan Calhoun, Charlie Glass, Eleanore Kennedy, Mary Link, Jennifer Maguire Isham,

Bettina von Hase, Chris Whittle, and Donna Wick for helping me to endlessly edit the text;

Mary Link, again, for keeping me sane and organized throughout this project;

Drs. Alexander Miller, Sasha Hilchuck, Kim Rosenthal, and Mark Davis

for answering my many calls and taking very good care of Luna in her final weeks;

and last but not least Chris Whittle, Maxi Moehlmann, Andrea Whittle, and Sasha Whittle

for being incredibly supportive while I finished this book.

PAGE EIGHTY-SIX:

LUNA, LOLA, PRISCILLA, AND CHRIS BY SASHA WHITTLE

PAGE NINETY-ONE:

LOLA ON PRISCILLA'S LAP BY MARY LINK

PAGE 101:

LUNA AND PRISCILLA BY NICHOLAS CALLAWAY

PAGES ELEVEN AND 110:

LUNA & LOLA LOGO BY MARTHA LINK WALSH

CALLAWAY
ARTS & ENTERTAINMENT

19 Fulton Street, Fifth Floor
New York, New York 10038

Printed in East Greenwich, Rhode Island by Meridian
Separations by Thomas Palmer

First Edition
10 9 8 7 6 5 4 3 2 1
Library of Congress Cataloging-in-Publication Data available.

ISBN: 978-0-935112-01-6

VISIT CALLAWAY AT WWW.CALLAWAY.COM.
READ MORE ABOUT LUNA AND LOLA AT WWW.LUNAANDLOLA.COM.

PRISCILLA RATTAZZI was born in Rome, Italy, and moved to the United States in 1974. She studied photography at Sarah Lawrence College and later worked as an assistant to the photographer Hiro. Through the late eighties, she was a fashion photographer; her work has appeared in such publications as *Brides, New York, Redbook, Self,* and the *New York Times Magazine* in the U.S. and *Vogue Italia, Donna,* and *Amica* in Italy. She is the author of four photography books: *Georgica Pond, Children, Best Friends,* and *Una Famiglia.* Over the past twenty years, there have been eight exhibitions of her work in New York, East Hampton, West Palm Beach, Knoxville, and Rome. Ms. Rattazzi lives with her family in New York and East Hampton.

FOR MORE INFORMATION, VISIT WWW.PRISCILLARATTAZZI.COM.